Ferocious
Selina Rodrigues

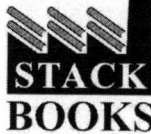

STACK
BOOKS

Smokestack Books
1 Lake Terrace,
Grewelthorpe,
Ripon HG4 3BU
e-mail: info@smokestack-books.co.uk
www.smokestack-books.co.uk

ISBN 9781838198855

Smokestack Books
is represented by
Inpress Ltd

Thanks are due to the editors of the following publications where some of these poems were first published: Helle Abelvik-Lawson, Anthony Hett and Laila Sumpton (eds) *In Protest, 150 Poems for Human Rights* (University of London, 2013), *Live Cannon Anthology 2020, Magma, Mslexia* and *South Bank Poetry*.

Heartfelt thankyous to the many colleagues and comrades and to the full-time, part-time and sometime artists.

For those who make trying work work.
And for those who believe
that writing about it is important.

Contents

High

Untitled

Push –
stone, seed, water

This is the effort you have made

Pull –
coin, gut, paper

This is the measure

of your cadence

Murmur

Her baby growls on waking
as the metal blinds rattle
in eagerness and Rahena clicks
fluorescents awake, stares at machines
and starts to count 10s, 20s, 50s
in her third brisk shop. Prepare
early. A last secret lorry rolls
through the city, she wonders
which floorboard gave slightly then,
a tendon of the building that pulls
and yields, whilst the curved palm
of moon fades in the lightening
and birds start to chatter.
A man wheels his cart
pausing, bending, collecting
and Rahena sees his lips move as if
he murmurs the morning.

Underneath it all

electricity loops around us, we are
deeper than skulls and mosaics,
than jewels. Clutter of a platform
trails away. Thoughts are thin
behind transport faces as we breathe
a newspaper's ink, sense warm hands
on metal. Who is the stranger now,
masked, or with lit cells.
We are careless, torn headlines
underfoot as we sway
westbound, your chest, my thigh
are all our bodies. Forget
the pre-paid minutes and miles.
Let's never arrive. Here it is –

containment. My mouth's
morning fur is as warm
as this tunnel. Even the stray bag
is tight within us. What is the danger
now. We dream of each other.
We want our rehearsed real fears.
Flecks on your shoulder
are to my lips. I trust you passenger,
no buds of conversation
opening around us. We are in awe
of the cave, held in arches
and in water as you sigh
in my ear. Our risk meaning
– nothing – anything – to me.

Every hour passing

Only ice-air awakens you.
A thought-beat as you pass the café.
The girl with shadowed eyes
is not on shift. The bus empty
but for Polish builders stretching
their fingers, final November leaves
misted by breath.

On time you spritz ylang-ylang
on the clients' outstretched wrists
and paint their skin for 10 hours.
The manager says grow your hair.
Only the blocks of beige light
warm the day. As you run
work spills from your bag - the ring

you borrowed, a snatched lipstick.
The driver mouths *no, no.*
Only the pulse of a Bajan voice
soothes the street. *Another bus hon,
sometime soon.* Smokers laugh
outside the cafe. Her brown cap
hides the cascading hair

you imagine, her eyes suggest
a small gift. A heart-jump,
but the queue is humming.
You eat on the run, arrive to clean
emptiness, to wipe tea-smears
from a desk, moisture from
a mouthpiece, and you don't see

anyone else. The 4th bus holds
the reflection of faces, lights.
Your fingers fret at the day –
the cards, keys. Only the hours
held you. Streetlights glare
too bright – but promise you
the relief of night.

Call Centre 1

The morning star, a key at my shoulder. At 5am I walked 6 miles to school. I was lucky that we could pay. My parents were bored of learning. I was their fifth. One day ma squeezed me through the window to pa to push his knees where he lay, and I unlocked the door. We say carry only enough for your journey. I was spat to town, then to city, then another. Always space for quiet ones. Now, even oldest sisters want me to call in my calls, at 10, 11, midnight. Could be our last talk, they say.

Lights waver
across the Bund
like thread
we are not afraid
of colour
at our feet
we cannot fear
the future
and the skyline
is my future.

High

A pinch of desire
at the breastbone.
Buildings rise
stacked close,
a triangle of breath
between them and nothing
is as elegant
as the sliding doors opening
to determined walls
oh muscular walls.
Black coat tails
slink ahead.

In the spine
of the building
speed fills our ears
through thirty floors.
Time to do, to do
to do, with a mouthful
of foam, and a jolt
of caffeine, with the double
tap of nails on the keys
and the keys.
9.5 hours
and counting.

Water bubbles
in the cooler. Morning
as tight as a stocking.
Take me Desi. There's a tangle
of cables. Let's –
darling, can you hear
my eyelashes click?
No columns, no screens
so powerfully high. Come
through the hundreds
of footsteps that walk
through the sky.

Fields, my fields

Here is my expanse. Here is your head,
your head, your head. Good morning.

Toss the cup and its last bitter grains
away as the copier heaves,

and we wake to our fields. Good day.
Upon the screen, documents unfold

like wings. Our light is programmed.
Smile for the formulas Jac.

Chew the paper Louise. Desmond
for a man you have beautiful nails

but ignore them – be trim
and cropped for keys. Rani, reap,

reap the numbers. No rolling coins,
no uncoiling graphs

in our files. Wipe the splatter
of gossip from your cheeks.

Daylight blooms now, inside.
Under low ceilings, here are your heads,

my landscape, my scene. With our palms'
first delicate sweat, our spines

curve to the screen. Around us cartwheel
the clicks and pings of machines.

Ferocious

Dear Boss. Today your head is full of rain.
Your husband wept, you scraped plates at 3am

and still brought pastries. We watch. You are kind.
Children run the office in your eyes,

they run your heart with laughter. Imagine.
We are all hands to this juddering system.

Aire Street's window is open a hair's-width
enough for you, a thin, steady breath.

As sun sparks day, my wired head turns.
Lambs are eating, dying, calling. It's the season

you say. *Leave early because now the earth
is open-mouthed and fields are torn for birth.*

So hours pass through us until I trip
down tilting floors into ferocious spring –

– the city's form – feathered grey, slash, drop blue
contained new buds. Dear Janie, away from you.

Rain falls again from untrustworthy skies. I need
the moors. For you, only commitment is right.

Call Centre 2

I never liked you my sister said before she flew 4,000 miles. But later, she rang. *I know you don't have much ready cash, but come when you can.* How can I visit the oil fields? *There's eight times the people in this city as Belfast. It's flat – and the heat* – she said *the office is smooth to touch, we don't even catch clouds in the glass.* When the fires burn in her head, at midnight, then she calls me.

Dreams smoke
thoughts spark
at the fires that
burned every day,
if not a boy or a shop
if not a pub or a girl.
Fall in love away
following a sister
who worked or
a cousin who sang daily
nightly to start again, visits
a return, to remember
to forget.

Guitars

Shshshh, Jac's losing the bars of his mind
beat thoughts swing out too loud, too far
scratching colleagues like the wired
plaintive calls of electric guitars.
Long bitten fingers tap a code
and yes, the cornet hums its refrain.
A printer shakes toner at his toes,
aaah-ooh he's forgotten to wash again.
Where are the songs? Such evenly-faced
people look and look away. Around him
the floors tilt, but Jac wants to notate
the jagged chirrup of the machines
to answer traffic's loose melody,
and open windows to bird-song that sweeps

through the room. Listen to bird-song that seeps
through Jac as he hums traffic's melody.
It's the winsome chirrup of the machine
he understands, but it's all discord
and as people shuffle and click around him
he tells the scanner, the next in three-four.
Ahhh shakala, Jac's not washed again,
old printer shakes toner at his toes.
While people stare, the sax calls his name
each day in the lift as he taps a code.
Oh the heart-trip notes of Spanish guitars
confuse those colleagues and the wires
of his thoughts stretch out too wide, too far.
Shshshh, Jac's finding the staves of his mind.

Perfection

You cut the ribbon, Janie.
At first, you opened the door.
Your eyes are wide now
but with neither hope
nor memory of rainy nights.
You unfold paper-chains.
Tasks are cards spread
over a table for choosing.
I used to feel that I knew you.

I've seen the white bureau
lined with books of code.
We used to play with wine,
laughed aloud at patterns,
kicked Jenga. Leaving a room
now your phrases flicker
like footprints alight.
Once, half-following a map
my calf tight from the clutch

I searched for a perfect view
of Cayton Bay til it was too late –
too dark – to stop. I think of you
this way now with hair
a curve of precision.
In small hours, I hold hands
with others but I kept your ring.
It was important at that time
I believe.

Moon Ascending

Ana says we have the moon ascending
and it's 5 years since Lucasz bled, spat, leaked,
bled and now she's here. This is our bar.
Ana nurses a Bloody Mary in remembrance.

Our boss is her second cousin twice removed,
that's why she floats in admin. Don't leave me
she cried. Should have gripped harder.
Legs like sawdust, the end of him flaking

in her hands. With that close-eyed smile she says
Lucasz grass-hopped studying plants in Greece.
She means island. As if there's no grass
in Romania. Ana wanted him to say kiss me

but he lost speech. Ana rings the astrology
helpline daily. At that, I want to touch her hand.

Call Centre 3

This will never be my real job. Sending orders to Paris, splicing
calls in Mumbai. It just works for now. This is my 5th country,
all legit, I've got papers. No coughs, no swallows, it's my voice
they want. I don't hear it crack, but sometimes the line breaks.
I'm thinking power-houses – Bangkok or maybe Frankfurt next.
When I can fly again. Sure sometimes my thoughts split, I lose
a call. 24 hours – a city's always your friend, right?

Circling
            bottom over
                        heels orders spin
in the power-houses
            want leaps
            through the night a demand
echoes in the small hours
            a wish
                        to you to you
voices approach
            and recede
  head-full, shoulder-
            cracked – are you the one –

Dispersed

Staples

Hot-house plants know
how to grow alone
      within the silver cells, creeping
in the after-hours, when lifts are anchored,
when stapled here,
      fingers to the desk
words are caught in the cylinders
      and pulses of the system, shooting
         to a screen, to a screen
as evening's warm hand
      smooths the office and breath
         returns through vents – stay,
         stay here, where there's order.

Replaying emails that came
      through the days, – who's in, who's out,
      who's finally out –
and it's all carefully measured,
an in-tray each, a bin beside desks,
      but careless in parts – visitors' stained cups
         in the white room, a jacket
         forgotten, its sculpted cuffs
      like an offering of flowers.
A signature pressed in a file
         and thoughts trapped
      in the machine, still rotating
         behind the toughened, smoked glass.

Handful of Men

Fingers of dune grass
strain towards the estuary.
Rain scatters
on the windscreen.
>Leave that Dev – leave
the car and constant
watching, amongst bricks
and thistle. The sea calls
come down.

A bird's print,
the waves' absence
on sand and cement.
A handful of men
>stoke the coughs
of smoke.
But abandonment is endless –
even this disintegration
won't end in a lifetime.

A gull sips sand-sticky water.
Signs are thrown
by the wind.
Music spirals the yard *I'll never*
>*leave...* and every nine hours
the shift turns.
In twos and threes they come
and go... *I have...*
clear-eyed, chosen men.

Here even mud sinks.
Here are hands
with tools and keys,
the lucky, unlucky men.
        Come down Dev. The sea holds
        a necklace of tin
        and nylon, a spray
        of mercury,
        its own counting waves.

Girl, Lost

Electricity sparks at my hands
from white desks and steel seams
as Rani giggles at time, plans
her uneven route whilst I sleep
we traded slammers
in a red-hearted bar
the un-told night she stayed over
I listened to her shower
she posts cochineal, puyaa
the real sights to me
in this terminal sky-scraper
that sways with engineering
she approaches the Andes and yet
I remember the print of her feet when wet.

Fingertips

Finger-tips check
for pins and blades
tug thread ends
and slip with sweat.
Price list, colour chart,
risk and roles
in a purposeful
tucked tie and shirt.
An everyday job
to quality control
the floors
as blood
pricks each row
and the factory flowers.

The factory flowers
in satin and lace
with the enduring trace
of rose-ammonia.
Drops, tints,
the constant stains
seep every day
through all our skin.
Twenty-four seven
rotas, lots
and shifts.
Incense
threads through cloth
and scents finger-tips.

Organza

Two seasons ahead. Satin and feathers
glisten in polythene sheets like wings
and rise to me through the invisible floors.

My skirt rustles. One mutters, one sings.
I pause and my fingers trace a stitch
dropped in Dhaka, a button lost in Beijing.

Crepe and tulle to slice and print.
Could you ever pause and be held
in velvet capes or upon the lace bibs.

This cuff for a breeze, this brim for clouds.
You sit in patterns as machines whirr
for our want, in the bright-dark shop fronts.

Autumn-Winter, you work hot-fingered.
I search beautiful racks but nothing fits
I tell you cold-faced, in Spring-Summer.

You tend the moleskin and finely-chewed silk
that shine and glint in everyday streets.
Chiffon and brocade. Your art and will
are the cuts and stitches that invite my body.

Distribution

The tread
of miles inside
begins. Eyes,
gloves, high-vis
bibs. Unpack
the day. Sortables
and oversize.
There's talk.
of cuts, always talk
I say. Open Dev's
divorce, roll-
over Lou's debts,
drink smoke
later. It's 14 hours
let's start.

An arm apart
at items.
A mile to tea.
The right price.
Think of what
the kids could be.
It'll be ok
with shelf
and shelf of want –
a coat, a phone,
rack and rack.
This is all packed
to be opened –
to please. We all
want that don't we.

Not you.
Salt, sugar
take us through.
They tick and
cross their lists.
Not you the boss
says come back
but not you.
Two in arms,
one sleeps open-
mouthed. Clothes, sprays,
perfume, screens.
Eyes run. The barcodes
dance. I worked so.
Choose me.

Plates

Welcome
please sit
glad you can eat
talk more
take a sip.

They want
a line, an eye
take from the left
he balances
give from the right

A trace of green
a knot of flesh
wine sings
all he wants to
feel is music

His evening
slips like a girl
from his sight
in the customers'
approach and flight

Exhales quick
flicks the butt
away inhales
5-minute break
in night chill.

Call Centre 4

Each other's other and we fought like cat and dog. Minger, minger I called as she walked upstairs in high heels. Once she threw the shoe back down. Once she sliced my shirt with nail file cuts, the rents too fine to stitch. We were born together, twins alive and different. I had to escape from sameness. Town to town, a stash of health and safety. A strong-arm face. I always get work.

Nights, I can't settle. Watching cameras watch empty floors. She married and I missed her. It didn't last and strangely, brought us together. Something to talk about. Now there is nothing I wouldn't tell her and do. We are childless and she cares. Wonders what a future could hold. I just miss occasional firmness, a man's breath. At 6am with a brandy, just one, we talk about my nights of security and hers of charts and needles.

Song

Sweetheart he
said, *how's my – a fish!*
did you? on TV now, oh
turn a minute, at work love
I'll be home – in a car! in a pool,
a quick call, how did she drink,
about seven, there's my girl
he sang each day as
we listened.

Desi smiled
in her green coat she
slept then, frogs, peas, everything
green she adores, as she burps,
he laughed as we typed, *I pretend to –*
hop, he should now, *my sleeping*
work as a team with *beauty*
and we all heard love
as he sang.

London Bridge

The swan bridge stretches and holds the tide
and streams of hurried, stray commuters.
A measured, silver wrap is at her side.

Lou undoes her cuffs and inhales powder.
Like ancient, herded sheep across a bridge
the numbers bunch and then disappear.

By day, at her desk the hundreds
of zeros run over the screen. She flicks
her fingers and shuffles the queen's head,

the queen's head. By night currencies slip
through other careless hands and Lou sighs
beside her low-slung, hollow bridge.

At last on a drift of powder she lies
bare-legged, with silt covering her toes.
The words repeat, I promise that I –

I promise to pay. Away from the rows
of digits and decimals, this water
takes trillions and endless zeros.

Louise bends towards white scurf and there
beneath the swan's wings, tastes the river.

Dispersed

You're everywhere now, that's the way it goes.
Where you exist, there's no locked door.
It's you, it's you, close examination shows

your freckles, your rings. And on each floor
in low-speaking rooms, you know a print
of you is sent from screen to screen. That flawed

love for a man closed your eyes, touched your lips.
Now, within steel and glass by the yucca's cool
assured tips you sit down. He nods you begin.

You report on impact, risk and control
whilst behind the desk that beautiful boss
and his distant wife in swimsuits, smile.

He lost his mind an instant. Your body is lost
and tumbles in cables. Small toes, a thigh
lie naked in stores. Your image is tossed

to the slice of machines and carefully filed.
There's nowhere to go, beyond the deep cache.
So close down and leave the staples of light
for the quiet, constant security staff.

Loose

Loose Change

With a forest of hair a man
sleeps through this concertina
of noise, a body-length away.
String ties his waist, cherries fall
from a bag. There's no garden
at Victoria. He keeps to a separate

private hour. Pesa, flous, cash
swirl in coffee. Computers wait
thin as leaves. Ties for each
Monday to Friday and flowered
on Fridays. We pay and throw
all loose change

to the pavement. Who trusts
their life to a chattering station –
sleeps with the pigeon's peck
of sushi, the tap of heels?
All hands are thought-filled.
His hair grows and knots and grows.

Borders

He is driving.
The mirror paints
the black road. No eyes
reflecting.

Fox-sharp, he can't be
sleeping as miles clip
to kilometres.

He is driving
through borders
and the blank language
of another country,

a grey-green morning
to a burnt afternoon.
Does he care what he carries?

He is driving.
No – yes – no. People
don't place yourselves
before him,

30 tons
and 12 heartbeats
covered

or is he driving
your home
to your house
pushing the axis

to a line. Dev was
a child
with a ball

on the street.
The moon balloons
then turns its back.
He is driving.

At Night Between

In the mean, last-train weather
with encrypted sticks
and downloads, after speeches
in the stamp
of tickets, deep in cartons,
check nails, pinch
creases, they know
where the alarms are.
Today's headlines
are on the floor.
Someone else's head
has rested here.

Too full of blank wine
and local cheese to sleep.
Quarter 2 targets,
Stages 3 and 4, minor
and serious breach
of contract repeat.
Conservatories pinned
against house
and house, doctored trees
spin by. Squares of light
but these towns
are too quick to read.

Horses stand
night-seeing. Slow
as men bend
in finger-work
to the track. E-mails
call to the tread
of routine, fingers
at the lap-top's mouth.
In the corridors
between office and hotel,
sit, think and click
fields and cells.

Call Centre 5

Single child, glad I was alone. Alone and full as a wood. No interference to my miles of reach. I snapped thoughts and ran, door unlocked and family sleeping behind. Opened my throat to birdsong. Blossom, snow, ants along my arms. Strange men? I've no mind to that. A cubicle and voices won't hold me. I run faster than myself and throw long shadows at sunset, no-one to call me home. Let the phones ring.

Turn
switch slam
locked clock
eyes waist
space health
safety key heat
map belt
up shshsh
focus.

Paragon Hotel

I wait on the pin-head
of a stool, the wind pushing, even here.
Come, once constant lover

as all day I rifle through visitors, the Paragon
station clock at my back
then wait again, under the spike of stars. Come

let's dance shoeless, under the five arches.
Smash hearts with me Janie. Let's up-end
this bar of its fossils and the bored words. Debts

and direction forgotten we'll walk away, a shower
of ourselves reflecting and spinning
under the expanding sky.

Cowgirl

It's work and sleep for you people
Lou says as the cowgirl cracks
another bottle. *How d'you do it?*
We work, the cowgirl says *and play*
with risks and glances in deep hours.
Her black hair shines.

It's work and work for some people.
Outside, the orchids' white
and orange throats curl. Hatless,
bandless, the cowgirl's black hair falls.
These folk must grip money
not let it run in the dark.

How do you sleep? From her bunk
she rises to fix the till. Single hairs
drift into the grits she cooks at 5,
the slammers she serves from noon.
With my eyes open, she says
whilst you dream of numbers, words.

Watching You Go

I don't know what I'm doing here. A strange
open thing to say. You don't usually speak
and we don't watch shadows fold and change
across our desks or mark the sun's gentle reach.
It's the afternoon hush and your voice is low.
You want to live in a different place,
to leave in spring, a delicate time to go,
to cross a border's paper-thin crease.
Elsewhere – beyond these keys and screens
go – open maps under mosaic roofs.
Learn new notes from score or memory
and sleep enveloped, as the proof
of paper cuts heal. Jac, in April's raw
spring light, open the day's atonal door